Reiki Raja Yoga

Reiki Raja Yoga

THE PHILOSOPHY AND PRACTICE OF HOLISTIC HAPPINESS AND SELF-REALIZATION

Shailesh Kumar

ISBN-13: 9781091275447

This book is dedicated to the Holy Absolute,
my Guru, Meera, and Kailash.
Thanks to Parul, Rajat, Vineet, Gaurav, Sunita,
Meredith, Payman, and all the initiates of the Divine Heart Center.

Contents

Preface

THERE IS EVIDENCE TO SUGGEST that our world and everything in it is a projection from a level of reality so beyond our own it is virtually beyond both space and time.

David Bohm, a leading 20th century quantum physicist, developed a new and controversial theory of the universe, a new model of reality that he called the Implicate Order. The theory of Implicate Order connects everything with everything else.

In principle, any individual element can reveal "detailed information about every other element in the universe." The central underlying theme of Bohm's theory is the "unbroken wholeness of the totality of existence as an undivided flowing movement without borders." Bohm says that the implicate order can just as easily be called spirit.

The Hindus call the implicate level of reality *Brahman*. *Brahman* itself formless, is the origin of all form in visible reality. In Hinduism this level of spiritual reality is composed of pure consciousness. Thus, consciousness is a subtler form of matter, more fundamental than matter itself. In Hindu cosmology, it is matter that has emerged from consciousness, and not the other way around. The physical world is virtually brought into being through the power of consciousness. The experience of Brahman is described as *Satchitananda. Satchitananda* is a compound Sanskrit word that is made up of:

- *Sat,* the eternal aspect of consciousness
- *Chit,* the comprehension or perceptive aspect of consciousness
- *Ananda,* pure bliss or happiness; the realization of life as pure bliss

Satchitananda is the ultimate experience of Divine. In this framework, spirit is the aspect of humanness that connects with the Absolute, Divine, or God.

There is an imposed contrast between the physical model of life developed by modern science orthodoxy (they too, were hunted as heretics, after all), and the spiritual conception of life, the soul, that lies at the foundation of many religious, philosophical, and mythological traditions.

Science gives a detailed account of limited aspects of a narrow slice of life. It strives for a description of life. The spiritual traditions strive to give life meaning. They do so by linking life with an additional, transcendental level of reality.

But that attempt brings in phenomena and categories of existence that seem at odds with or are ineffectively contained within the framework of empirical science. There's "stuff" we haven't quite figured out how to measure yet.

Questions naturally arise about the precise location of truth along this vector.

Religious traditions are often criticized for providing untestable constructs in their explanations of phenomena. Among these debated constructs, foremost may be the existence of a soul. But is the concept of soul really so equivocal and is it necessarily so antagonistic to empirical evidence?

According to the Standard Model of Particle Physics, atomic nuclei are made up of smaller particles called protons and neutrons, which are themselves made up of hadrons. Hadrons are a composite of yet more fundamental particles called quarks which can never be observed in nature. In fact, the color confinement phenomenon states that color charged particles such as quarks cannot be isolated singularly, and therefore can never be directly observed. Quarks may only be observed at the Hadron level.

Nevertheless, they were postulated in 1964 by Gell-Mann and Zweig and are widely accepted by the physics community. Yet, all experiments validating the existence of the quarks have produced only indirect proof of their existence.

Experiments that confirm the existence of quarks never involve direct observation and such observation is never demanded as part of the proof of their existence. That's fact. Therefore, detection of influence with no expectation of direct detection is certainly a valid way to confirm existence in science.

Vedic philosophy describes another type of particle called the *atman*. In Sanskrit *atman* means soul or eternal self. The *atman* has different properties from those of ordinary particles. Unlike ordinary matter and anti-matter particles, the *atman* has four properties:

- Eternality
- Individuality
- Knowledge
- Bliss

The Eternality property means that the *atman* does not come into or go out of existence. It does not decay or degrade. It is always present and it maintains its individuality. It cannot be decomposed. It's unchangeable.

The Individuality property means that the *atman* does not unite with other particles to create more complex structures, nor does it merge with others. The *atman* does not interact directly with matter, but given that the *atman* is the source of consciousness and the life force in any living entity, any entity, whether human, animal, or plant, displaying consciousness or life force reveals the presence of an *atman*.

The living are not composed of *atmans*; they are *atmans*. The living are virtually animating the material bodies that encase them. As soon as the *atman* leaves one body for another, the old body no longer exhibits consciousness or life signs and begins to degrade and chemically recombine.

Knowledge refers to the *atman's* cognizance of its source, its interactions with the source, and its constitutional position.

Bliss refers to the *atman's* natural state of joy in the service of Divine.

Remember, these are names for concepts. If they sound strange, change them. That's all English can manage in its arsenal of words. Eskimos have twelve words for snow! We only have two. We don't have too many words for our spiritual frameworks and we sure are not looking for new ones and the ones we do have, trigger all sorts of reactions in most people that can often get in the way of the principle points. Substitute other technical or spiritual words, if you need to.

To declare that there is no soul, just because we can't directly see it with our current instruments, is akin to saying that there are no quarks because we can't detect them directly in our labs. Both the soul and the quarks' existence can be inferred indirectly by their effects. That is, particle interactions in the case of the quarks; living symptoms and consciousness in the case of what we today call soul because that's its name for now (call it something else if that name seems controversial).

There is, however, a method for directly perceiving the soul or eternal self; it involves using the mind as a type of mirror, so that the conscious mind may experience the soul using spiritual senses. To do this, the mind must first be cleansed of all selfishness, cruelty and ego. That's the ritual practice.

This is the goal of Reiki Raja Yoga in a nutshell, to apply techniques that remove blockages and imbalances in the chakras (we'll get to them in a bit), and to focus, tame, and purify the mind.

Reiki Raja Yoga is a union of two ancient practices, one a healing system, the other a meditative system. The practice of Reiki Raja Yoga cultivates holistic happiness and self-realization.

In the first stage, you elevate your mind and bring it to the level of the soul. In the next stage, you elevate your soul and bring it to the level of spirit. In the final stage, you untangle your spirit and become one with the Divine—you become self-realized or enlightened.

This book introduces you to the practice of Reiki Raja Yoga.

This book is in part about Reiki. The practice works to eliminate your personal energy blocks, which in turn elevates your mind, bringing it to the level of soul. In this way, Reiki brings about holistic happiness.

Reiki is a Japanese technique that was rediscovered in the 20s. Look it up. Reiki helps to restore harmony in the mind, body and spirit.

Life force energy flows through our subtle bodies along pathways and chakras. When energy flows freely, we experience health and well-being. Conversely, when energy flow is disrupted or restricted, we are more vulnerable to illness. Reiki consists of positioning your hands on your body, with or without touch. It concentrates on the chakras, energy centers along the spine, and on the main internal organs.

The book is also about Raja Yoga. Self-realization begins by becoming aware of one's state of mind. It is through awareness that one learns to calm the mind and bring it to a single point of focus. It is at this point that we direct our attention inward, toward our true nature. Our true nature is Divine.

Here, Reiki and Raja Yoga work together synergistically. Raja Yoga increases the flow of Reiki energy in your life. Raja Yoga also helps you understand the underlying spiritual force behind Reiki in a deeper way.

Once you commit to the practice of Reiki Raja Yoga, everything else begins to fall into place and the universe begins to align with you.

You may not have access to a particle accelerator to prove for yourself the existence of quarks; but you can prove to yourself the existence of the soul and processes that take you closer to it. Reiki Raja Yoga, brings happiness and inner fulfillment. Its transformative power truly enhances your life and positively influences the lives of those around you.

"There is a light in this world, a healing spirit more powerful than any darkness we may encounter. We sometimes lose sight of this force when there is suffering, too much pain. Then suddenly, the spirit will emerge through the lives of ordinary people who hear a call and answer in extraordinary ways."

–*Sir Richard Attenborough*

Why Practice Reiki Raja Yoga?

SRI YUKTESHWAR GIRI, A KRIYA yogi, and the Guru of Paramahansa Yogananda said: "Everything in the future will improve if you are making a spiritual effort now." So, the short answer is, you practice Reiki Raja Yoga because that effort will directly improve your physical and spiritual life.

There is an infinite spiritual field that is present everywhere with an inexhaustible power to heal. Reiki Raja Yoga teaches you to tap into this field to heal yourself and achieve holistic happiness and self-realization.

Holistic happiness is a state of physical, emotional, and spiritual health that permeates all aspects of your life from your relationships to your financial well-being. When your body, mind, and spirit are happy at once.

This book introduces ancient meditation techniques in a unique way designed to make powerful and demanding spiritual practices fit into today's jam-packed and busy lifestyles.

Seekers of every era, whether spiritual or scientific, expended effort to uncover the mysteries of consciousness or the mysteries of the universe.

We are living in a spiritually meaningful era. Each era has its planetary challenges. The challenge of this era is to unravel human consciousness with unprecedented intensity in order to achieve greater good for all humanity.

"Divine union is possible through self-effort, and is not dependent on theological beliefs or on the arbitrary will of a Cosmic Dictator."

–*Lahiri Mahasaya*

How Reiki Raja Yoga Works

All transformations need power to manifest. In Reiki Raja Yoga, there are two Divine powers that make holistic happiness possible. These are *Bhakti,* the Power of Devotion, and *Shakti,* the Power of Divine Will. When you are devoted and exercise your will positively, you bring about *Kripa* or Divine Grace, which in turn harnesses the unlimited power of Divine Will.

By learning to tap into these universal powers, then doing so regularly, you can transform your body, mind, and spirit not only to experience holistic happiness yourself, but to transmit and bring it to others.

When your experience of holistic happiness becomes permanent, it is called *Ananda.* It is said that in this state you first experience the Absolute directly and begin your journey into self-realization.

Reiki Raja Yoga recognizes a direct relationship between your personal energy and the Universal Energy System and teaches you how to strengthen it and use it effectively to fuel your personal transformations.

Devotees of the deity *Hanuman* sing verses from the Tulasi Das's version of the *Ramayana* in *Hanuman*'s praise. These tell of selfless exploits and total devotion to Lord *Rama*, of how *Hanuman* leapt across the ocean to destroy *Lanka* and flew back holding the medicine mountain that healed the mortally wounded *Lakshmana*.

Hanuman, the *Mahavir*, the greatest warrior, is the embodiment of *Shakti* and *Bhakti*. When you discover holistic happiness and experience self-realization, you become *Mahavir* or the most powerful of warriors and yogis.

Reiki Raja Yoga combines meditation techniques to generate devotion in your heart and instill a positive will power in your mind.

A heart full of love and a mind full of will can ensure that you have the power to create soul-healing actions that enable holistic happiness. This path guides you to skillfully and effortlessly maneuver the two powers of the Absolute into your life.

While holistic happiness is an objective state, happiness is subjective. Different people need different things to make them happy. Reiki Raja Yoga supports the pursuit of holistic happiness based on your definition of happiness. For you, inner happiness may be more important than the happiness of material accomplishments. Or you may still desire material achievements to make you happy. This path supports both pursuits—the pursuit of inner happiness regardless of outward circumstances, as well as the pursuit of happiness through worthwhile material achievements.

You can learn to connect to spiritual fields that can help dissolve and burn down your energy blocks also called karmic blocks. Once your karmic blocks are burned away you attract holistic happiness which in turn speeds up your spiritual evolution.

The ultimate state of spiritual evolution is *Satchitananda*, which means conscious existence in eternal bliss. *Sat* or eternal consciousness is the essence of life or the amount of life that is inside you. *Chit* is the peaceful, complete, and unbroken consciousness of you being life itself and not simply who you happen to be in this life. *Ananda* is pure bliss or the essence of life, the realization that life itself is bliss.

The seeker or apprentice in Reiki Raja Yoga oscillates between happiness and sorrow states. After practicing this ancient meditation, a more stable inner and outer state is achieved. After years of regular practice, holistic happiness manifests in your life. *Satchitananda* is realized after a lifetime of practice, unflinching faith, surrender, and determined effort. It is the innate nature of the Absolute.

This book provides access to innovative and practical techniques to encourage physical, emotional, mental, and spiritual healing.

The basic meditations described in this book help you to start your spiritual journey and assists in your journey of self-discovery, empathy, awareness, personal growth, and spiritual progress.

The intent is to take you forward in your journey toward self-realization.

You will understand the root cause of the condition we call unhappiness, as we introduce the concepts of aura, chakras, vastu, and energy, so that you can eradicate energy barriers to health, progress, including material progress, relationships, and knowledge.

We help you understand this powerful spiritual practice (*sadhna*) that combines the path of self-effort (*shram*) and surrender (*samarpan*).

The path of Reiki Raja Yoga transforms you from inside through a series of non-denominational spiritual practices.

You do not have to believe in any particular faith or God to harness the power of Reiki Raja Yoga. It is more about your connection with a higher power or the Absolute, as it makes sense to you.

"Your religion is not the thoughts and beliefs in which you enclose yourself, but the garment of light you weave around your heart. Discover who you are, behind those outer trappings, and you will discover who Jesus was, and Buddha, and Krishna. For the masters come to earth for the purpose of holding up to every man a reflection of his deeper, eternal Self."

–*Paramahansa Yogananda*

The Pursuit of Spirituality

IN ORDER TO MAKE YOUR holistic happiness eternal, you must ensure that a deep pursuit of spirituality is an integral part of your life.

Think of spirituality as the inclination of a mind to know more about itself and in the recognition of the self as an unlimited spirit.

Your happiness depends on how well you know yourself. When you don't know your true self, you only use a fraction of your mind's power and your decision making suffers. Your decisions become based on fear or cultural and social conditioning.

This limited state of the mind is called *avidya* or spiritual ignorance. There is a subtle limiting collective principle in creation that hides your true identity from your conscious mind. It is called *maya* or cosmic hypnosis.

Spirituality is the practice of unfolding yourself layer-by-layer to ultimately realize the inexhaustible spirit overflowing with pure unlimited love and dazzling with infinite intelligence. When you begin to see glimpses of your unlimited and infinite self, you feel less fearful, less stressed, more loving, and more frequently happy. And then, you develop the power to spread this happiness around yourself, fostering happiness within your world and worldwide.

Raja Yoga is the "yoga of the mind." You learn to use the mind to objectively observe the world around you and to understand its transitory yet clinging nature. You turn the mind inward to probe the nature of ego. Ego or *ahamkar* or pride about oneself is the root of all unhappiness. When you learn to make these inner and outer observations with patience and objectivity, you understand how your ego can create an incorrect self-image and limit your happiness.

"If you want to find the secrets of the universe, think in terms of energy, frequency and vibration."

–*Nikola Tesla*

Energy Management

WE ARE ALL INFUSED WITH a universal energy that nourishes and connects life. Humans are surrounded by a field comprised of this energy. It has been called by various names, such as *prana*, and *chi*.

Each life process in your body, mind, and spirit, how your mind functions, how you express emotions, your physical body's operating system, all are supported by this energy field. Infinite love, unlimited consciousness, infinite health, power, wellness, and knowledge are all born from this field of pure consciousness.

This is conscious energy that is connected with the higher energy of the universe. It is the linkage between the physical and spiritual worlds.

Life Energies

There are three kinds of energies that impact your happiness:

- Personal energy
  The energy necessary for your personal well-being.
- Social energy
  The energy of people with whom you interact with daily.
- Spatial energy
  The energy of the space that you live in.

Personal Energy

Your personal energy is made up of

- The Aura
- The Chakra System

The aura is an energy field that surrounds and extends out of your physical body. It is generated by the chakras, seven vortices of energy spinning inside your body along your spine. We'll discuss this all in more detail in the next few chapters.

Social Energy

Social energy is the energy of the people whom you interact with every day.

A biological research team at Bielefeld University in Bielefeld Germany made a groundbreaking discovery showing that plants can draw an alternative source of energy from other plants. People draw energy from others in much the same way.

Emotions such as fear, anger, and frustration are energies. You can potentially "catch" them from people without realizing it. If you tend to be an emotional sponge, it's vital to know how to avoid taking on an individual's negative emotions or the free-floating kind in crowds.

Another twist is that chronic anxiety, depression, or stress can turn you into an emotional sponge by wearing down your defenses. Suddenly, you become hyper-attuned to others, especially those with similar pain.

From an energetic standpoint, negative emotions can originate from several sources. What you're feeling may be your own; it may be someone else's; or it may be a combination of both.

How can you tell the difference?

First, ask yourself: Is the feeling mine or someone else's? It could be both. For instance, if you've just watched a comedy, yet you came home from the movie theater feeling blue, you may have incorporated the depression of the people sitting beside you; in close proximity, energy fields overlap.

What highly sensitive people need to do is learn how to manage their personal energy and be aware of the social energy around them.

Spatial Energy

The energy levels predominant in your working space (factory, shop, or office) and living space (home) play an influential role in your daily life. As a result, they have a direct impact on your personal and professional life.

These energy levels are termed spatial energies or vastu energies in Sanskrit and are influenced by:

- Inner and outer vastu and feng shui
- Five elements (the panchtatvas or the panchmahabhutas)
- The influence of the nine planets
- The cosmic energy of the place

Spatial energy can be termed a combination of all the above factors.

The value of spatial energy is determined by the positivity and negativity of the above-mentioned factors.

In a scenario where the spatial energy is positive, the individuals living in that space receive positive energy through their chakras and auras. This brings in loads of health, happiness, and spiritual harmony.

When the spatial energy is negative, the individuals become recipients of negative energy and therefore experience suffering and unhappiness.

There are techniques to either enhance the already positive spatial energy or transform the negative energy into positive energy.

Vastu Healing

Vastu healing is the healing of the space where one lives. This is done using powerful instruments or yantras, such as gem stones, pyramids, and Rudraksha beads, to improve the spiritual and mental energy field of your home, office, shop, and other premises.

These yantras use ancient principles of vastu and modern science of spiritual and mental energy management. For example, powerful yantras can attract and enhance the flow of material energies (golden energies) and help in improving the finances of a household or an organization. They can help improve overall abundance. The use of yantras can also improve the financial inflows or sales for businesses. The yantra directly interacts with the aura or bioenergy fields of a person or with the spatial energy or oorja of the premises. It can rectify the deficiency of spiritual and mental energies and can plug leaks in the energy fields that are the cause of the depletion of energies.

"Every man is the builder of a Temple
called his body, nor can he get off by
hammering marble instead."

–*Henry David Thoreau*

The Aura

EVERYTHING IN THE UNIVERSE VIBRATES. Every atom, part of an atom, electron, proton, and neutron vibrates. Recall that consciousness evolves into matter and is more fundamental than matter itself. Consciousness is vibrationless existence. Your thoughts are vibrations, and these vibrations create energy fields called the aura. The aura penetrates and engulfs the physical body and extends beyond it.

Aura is a Western term. In yogic scripture, humans have five koshas or sheaths in their body. These are:

1. *Annamaya* kosha—physical sheath
2. *Pranmaya* kosha—energy sheath
3. *Manomaya* kosha—emotional sheath
4. *Gyanmaya* kosha—mental/intellectual sheath
5. *Anandmaya* kosha—causal sheath or the radiance of the soul

The second, third, and fourth koshas make up the human aura. For simplicity, some western teachings consider all five to be the aura.

In Reiki Raja Yoga, your aura is the energy field projected by your chakras.

An aura is made up of astral lights and energies. In the same manner as visible light, it consists of a spectrum of colors. Aura colors exist on the astral plane and so cannot normally be seen with the naked eye. The colors are "felt" through the third-eye chakra when it has become active through practice. Eventually, with enough practice an active third-eye chakra may empower the physical eyes so the practitioner can see astral colors like normal colors.

The aura of inanimate objects is fixed and can only be altered by conscious intent. The aura around conscious beings, however, varies with time, sometimes quickly and sometimes slowly. The aura changes in size and colors depending on your emotional state and so can match the endless changes in thoughts and emotions.

Generally, the aura is enhanced through loving and happy thoughts and diminished through angry and sad thoughts.

All aura concepts try to evaluate and classify this energy continuum that is beyond your physical body. Your various mental states extend to and affect this energy continuum. Thus, your aura is a reflection of your true state of mind

Extent and Brightness

Your aura adjusts its size according to many factors, including population density where you live. Negative thoughts and emotions such as fear, grief, and anger, as well as physical illness weaken your connection with the universe and can reduce both the quality and size of your aura.

In Hindu scriptures, it is said that spiritual masters have auras that extend from hundreds of feet to miles. As the masters' consciousness evolves and expands, their aura becomes limitless as it merges with the universal aura.

Your aura, especially its color and intensity around your head is effectively your spiritual signature. Spiritual progress cleans and brightens the auras. Spiritual and physical health results in uniform energy distribution in the aura. Conversely, a dark or gray aura demonstrates unclear intentions and a blocked spirit. Most people are not even aware of their aura.

Practicing Reiki Raja Yoga allows you to come to a realization of your aura. Reiki Raja Yoga techniques also spiritually heal your aura, thus allowing you to affect your destiny.

The Meaning of the Colors

Most people have one or two predominant colors in their aura. These colors are often their favorite colors.

In addition to these colors, auras also demonstrate the presence of flashes, flames, or clouds. These reflect desires, thoughts, feelings, and energy blocks.

Energy blocks in your aura can deplete your physical body. And make you feel tired for no reason and create experiences of hardship or blocks in life despite making efforts.

It is important to note that these are not physical colors but are sensed intuitively by spiritual masters or healers through their third eye which senses the color and the spiritual or material element in the color.

Purple

Spiritual thoughts give rise to purple in the aura. Darker purples represent a rational understanding of spirituality. Lighter purple, or white highlights within indicate faith; such a person experiences the Absolute spontaneously through faith rather than complicated logic. Changes in purple from dark to bright to white represent a journey from rationality to faith.

Indigo

Represents wisdom and intuition.

Blue

The color of sky represents expansion in empathy, a mature understanding of the world. Patience and peace bring about blue.

Green

Signifies joy and healing and indicates natural healing ability. Restful, joyful, healing energy brings about bright green. Most natural healers have a green strong point in their aura.

Yellow-Gold

Represents material achievement and knowledge. The power of achievement and ability to acquire knowledge. Abundant life-force energy creates a golden halo around the head. A fully active back third-eye chakra with accumulated pranic energy creates a golden halo.

Orange

Creativity and passion; passion to achieve life purpose bring about orange. Renunciant monks in India wear orange or saffron colored robes to balance the passionate aspect of their human nature and to direct their creativity and passion toward spiritual purpose.

Red

Materialistic thoughts and thoughts about the physical body bring about red. A red aura indicates a materialistic person with a strong will to live. Strong red color shows a person who believes only that which can be physically seen.

Pink

Spiritual love creates pink. A pink aura comes about when a perfect balance between spirituality and materialism is achieved. The presence of Reiki in the aura creates pink.

Strengthening Your Aura

As you remember that your aura also influences the things and people you come in contact with along with impacting your own personality, you understand the need to develop a strong aura.

Reiki and Raja Yoga offer specific techniques that can enable you to strengthen your aura. You may directly change your aura with vibrations by holding in your mind clear, distinct pictures of desirable feelings and objects while meditating.

It also helps to visualize a flow of brilliant white light flooding the aura like a waterfall from the top of your head to the base of your feet, cleansing all the blocks and balancing the abnormalities in the aura.

The Aura and Chakras

The aura is generated by the chakras. Think of it as the projection of chakra energy. We'll talk about chakras next.

The Chakra System

YOUR BODY HAS PHYSICAL SYSTEMS such as your organs, nervous system, glands, muscles, bones, and vascular system. In addition to those, your body possesses a subtle energy system through which vital life-force energy flows. This system comprises energy bodies that engulf your physical body and help you to process emotions, thoughts and ideas.

Each energy body is associated with an energy center called a chakra. Chakras work like valves that allow this energy to pass through your spiritual, mental, physical, and emotional being.

There are seven major chakras in the chakra system. Think of the chakras as seven vortices of energy spinning inside your body along your spine, from the bottom of your pelvis to the crown of your head. The chakras along this axis act as a seven-step connection between life and the field of pure consciousness energy.

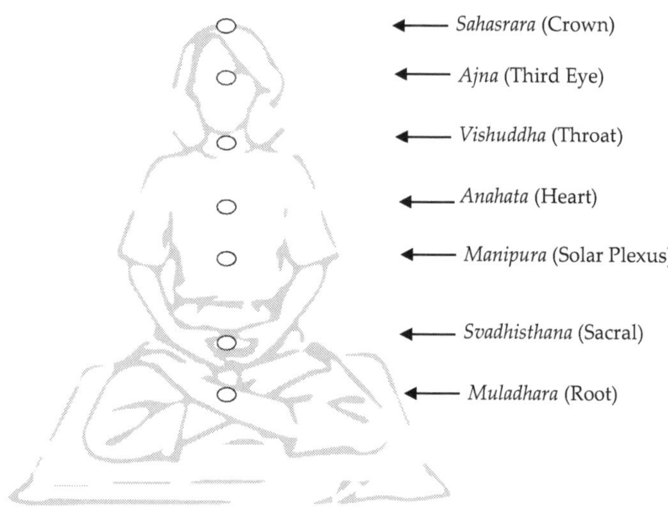

This energy manifests unlimited potential and infinite power, both natural attributes of all spiritual beings. The Chakra System directs and regulates how prana or the life force exists within your body's field and manifests itself in your physical life.

The Root Chakra: Safety, Survival, Security

Located inside the sushumna nadi, at the base of the spine, the root or *muladhara* chakra is your foundation or earth chakra. Close to the pubic bone and facing down toward your feet, it lays the energy foundation of your body. Your feelings related to safety, survival, and security emerge from this center.

People with a closed root chakra endlessly twist their ankles, experience foot or hip pain, don't practice healthy habits, and would have difficulty with most basic yoga positions. You procrastinate, you're always defensive, you are afraid.

A healthy root chakra connects you to the earth and makes you comfortable in your own skin. Self-confidence and strong health come from a balanced root chakra.

The Sacral Chakra: Passion, Desire, Pleasure

Four to six finger widths above the root chakra, and below the level of the navel, is the sacral or *svadhisthana* chakra. The seat of your lower self and home of instant gratification, it drives your ego's immediate goals.

The chakra of self-acceptance allows you to adapt to change in your life. It's the focal point of creativity, movement, sexuality, and emotions. This chakra empowers a woman to create life and drives the creative self. It's the center of immediate objectives and desires and anything that satisfies your average ego.

An imbalance or block in this chakra leads to questions like "what am I doing," or "what should I do next?" Guilt and emotional detachment, over criticism of your current state of health or even financial state are rooted here. Inability to lose weight despite all attempts and methods may be rooted in this chakra.

A healed and balanced sacral chakra allows you to express your passions and emotions creatively without them overtaking your life.

The Solar Plexus Chakra: Seat of Power to Achieve

Located inside the sushumna nadi, at the level of the solar plexus, is the solar or *manipura* chakra where your power to achieve springs.

The lure of this chakra, both on the material and the astral planes, is so intense that it can prevent you from advancing to higher chakras. Like a fire that burns whatever is thrown into it, and asks for more, this is the energy center that can send you on a life-long pursuit of status. Poor appetite and unexpected weight gain, indigestion, constipation and irritable bowls all originate here.

A balanced solar chakra brings courage, power and humility.

The Heart Chakra: Unconditional Love

Located inside the sushumna nadi, at the level of the heart, is the heart or *anahata* chakra. Your heart chakra draws joy from the universe from the back and projects love from the front. This is the middle chakra with the three worldly chakras below it and the three spiritual chakras above. The heart chakra is the connection between the two sides and allows you to balance your spiritual qualities with your physical.

A closed heart chakra can result in a lack of compassion or empathy. Physically, it can result in blocked arteries, and heart disease.

A balanced heart chakra lets you love deeply, fully, and sincerely both yourself and others.

The Throat Chakra: Patience, Empathy, Self-Expression

Located inside the sushumna nadi, at the level of the throat, is your throat or *vishuddha* chakra, the seat of patience, understanding, and self-expression. A healthy and balanced throat chakra allows you to bear the brunt of all the negativity thrown your way by the physical world and yet continue to express, communicate and create with your voice. It empowers you to speak truth and gives you the patience to hear truth.

Blocks in the throat chakra can lead to compulsive lying, and inability to express your thoughts effectively, to stammer and stumble, or remain silent. Creative blocks and a lack of inspiration may be seated in this chakra.

Balance in your throat chakra leads to purification of ideas and transformation of the world around you.

The Third Eye Chakra: Self Knowledge, Spiritual Genius

Located inside the sushumna nadi, between the eyebrows, is the third eye or *ajna* chakra. Ajna is Sanskrit for command

and the third eye chakra is the command center of the mind and body.

Where an open solar plexus chakra allows material accomplishments, the open third eye manifests spiritual genius.

The focal point of self-knowledge, the third eye allows you to perceive things not detectable by the conscious mind or what we call intuition. It fills the mind and body with deeper knowledge about the world and the self. This is where your aspirations and dreams live.

Self-doubt is commonly associated with a blocked third eye chakra, as are sinus and tension headaches. An overactive third eye induces jealousy and disagreement.

A balanced third eye keeps you grounded in the body and in the world then balances the reactions of your intellect as well as your feelings toward the outside world.

The Crown Chakra: Pure Awareness

Located at the top of your head and extending out is the seat of your universal self, the crown or *sahasrara* chakra. This is the center of wisdom, self-realization and pure consciousness.

People with a closed crown chakra have little or no interest in the spiritual so if you're reading this book chances are your crown chakra is beginning to open. Personal tragedies can often affect this chakra.

A balanced crown chakra imparts a sense of spirituality and of connectedness in yourself and the world around you.

The Nadis

According to ancient Indian scriptures, there are 72,000 nadis. As mentioned earlier, the chakra system directs and regulates how *prana* or the life force exists within your body's field. The *prana* flows in and out of the body through the chakras as well as the *nadis*. While chakras are energy vortices inside your body, the *nadis* are energy channels running along your body. The Chinese refer to *nadis* as energy meridians which function like a river, carrying energy through your body, nourishing it, and balancing your physical system, mental function, and spiritual purpose. This book teaches exercises that focus on the three most important nadis through which prana flows. These are called sushumna, ida, and pingala.

Sushumna

The *Sushumna nadi* begins at the first chakra and ends at the seventh. It is the body's most important energy channel because it carries *kundalini* energy from the base of the spine to the crown of the head, imparting self-realization. It pierces through each chakra's center, extending from the base of the spine to the crown of the head.

Ida and Pingala

There are two other *nadis* that wrap themselves around the *sushumna nadi*. They are called the *ida* and the *pingala nadis* and are present around each chakra.

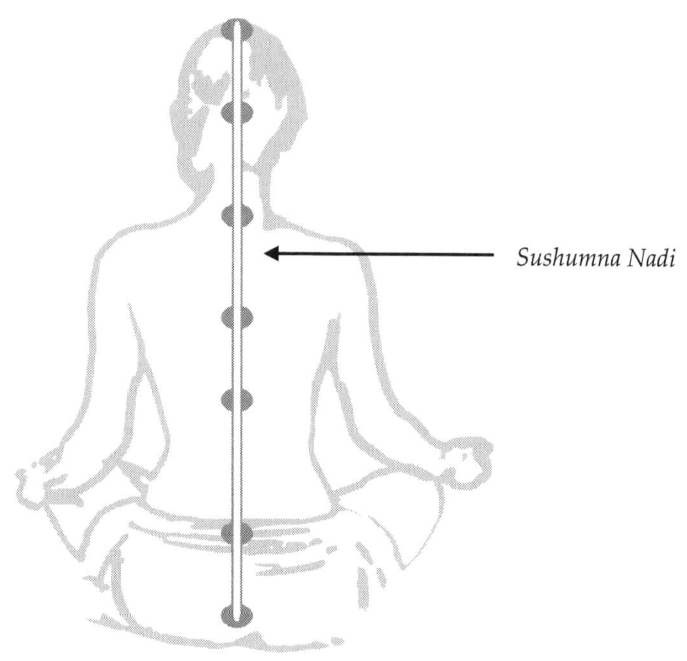

Ida conducts a cooling, calm receptive and meditative energy or what the Chinese call yin. *Pingala* conducts a heating, active, forceful, get-it-done energy or yang in Chinese philosophy. *Ida* energy can calm an overloaded chakra and *pingala* energy can energize a blocked chakra.

Exercises such as *pranayama* breathing later in this book show how to tap into the flow within *ida* and *pingala* and fill your body with appropriate *prana* energy.

The practice of Reiki Raja Yoga harmonizes and blends into one the multiple intelligences of all the chakras thus bringing about yoga.

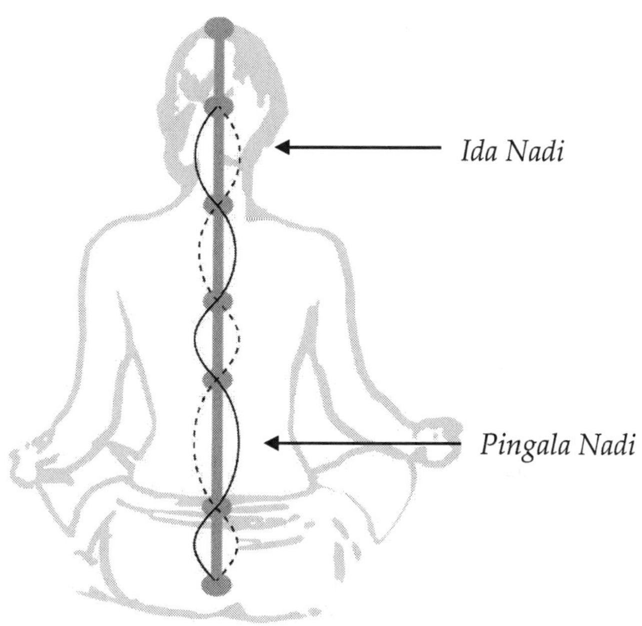

Sensing and Opening your Chakras

You can scan your energy body to sense how your chakras are moving and acting. You can get better attuned to your chakras and learn to feel, evaluate, and heal them. Some of the exercises in the Exercises chapter show you how to accomplish that.

"The self-controlled person, moving among objects, with senses free from attachment and malevolence and brought under control, attains tranquility."

–*The Bhagavad Gita*

Karma

THE WORD KARMA MEANS WORK, deed, or action, and describes actions as well as their resultant energy. Karma governs our environment and our physical and spiritual inheritance. From a karmic perspective, life is a specific amount of energy directed by a specific amount of information.

According to karmic law, the world unfolding before you today is a reflection of your past, and how you act today creates your future. Karma determines everything that you experience. Every thought, feeling, and event has been created specifically to help you learn in the present things you have not resolved or learned in your past.

Swami Paramahansa Yogananda teaches that habits cultivated in your past lives, materially and substantially create your physical, mental, and emotional makeup in this life. You have forgotten those habits, but they have not forgotten you. Your karma comprises all your past thoughts, actions, and habits. It follows you through the crowded centuries of your experiences and with each rebirth, creates your physical form and your personality.

These individually woven past-life patterns make one person different from another and fashion the great variety of human appearances and characteristics. We are all different because karma determines the manner in which information is fed into our system.

Karmic learning and the observation of suffering in the world is a universal mechanism that over many lives completes your knowledge of the world. Unfolding karma allows you to view life from different perspectives and enables you to think about and correct your mistakes.

The shape of your character is dependent on the "karmic data" that has gone into you at birth. You carry with you into your current birth a folder of your past experiences. Into what sort of nation were you born; what was going on there at the time of your birth; what religious and ethnic background, what "tribe," and into what sort of cultural reality were you born? What sort of education did you receive, what sort of values surrounded you? All of these are driven by the "karmic data" imprinted into your causal body or *karana sarira* and are what leads to your life as you find it.

In Hinduism, there are three types of karma:

- *Sanchita*
- *Prarabdha*
- *Kriyamana*

Sanchita karma is the totality of your karma present at your birth and responsible for all your rebirths that goes back through all time to original creation. It is not possible to endure all of that karma in one lifetime without dying. So, creation, out of compassion, allots each individual only a portion of his or her karma to manage in a single lifetime.

Prarabdha karma is that portion of your *Sanchita* karma allotted to you for this lifetime. It's the karma that is ready for you to tackle and understand.

There are two subcategories of *Prarabdha*:

- *Sthaanbaddh*
- *Samaybaddh*

Sthaanbaddh karma manifests only in a particular place. For example, when you go to a particular place, you always get sick or are confronted with great upheaval and when you return, everything returns to normal.

Samaybaddh karma manifest only at or after a certain time. Everything seems to be going well in life and then suddenly after a particular year, everything seems to fall apart or turn around and suddenly become amazing. You are often left to figure out how things fell apart or be in awe of how things turned around.

Finally, there is *kriyamana* karma, which is the karma you produce in your current life and the way your actions and thoughts in this life contribute to your *sanchita* karma.

Sanchita karma is like a savings account of karma. From the sanchita savings account, you can spend your prarabdha karma. The kriyamana karma is the cash you have in your pocket.

Reiki Raja Yoga allows you to dissolve and thereby alter your karma. Through the meditation and healing techniques of Reiki Raja Yoga, your past karma works out at a faster pace than it normally would. Therefore, any opposing force exerted by your karmic destiny on your free will is reduced. The amount of karma you dissolve depends on the intensity of your daily practice. You then experience your life in line with what you desire your life to be, achieving holistic happiness and progressing into self-realization.

Awakening the Kundalini

Kundalini is a manifestation of divine will or *shakti.* It is an energy located in the base of the spine that in one of its manifestations sustains the physical body and its functions from within the *muladhara* or root chakra.

Hindu scripture describes three expressions of the *kundalini*:

- *Para-kundalini*
  The first expression is unmanifested cosmic energy.
- *Prana-kundalini*
  The second expression is the vital energy of the created universe.
- *Shakti-kundalini*
  The third expression is consciousness itself. *Shakti kundalini* is the intermediary between the other two expressions of *kundalini.*

Shakti kundalini is the eternal foundation of bliss flowing from the *sahasrara* (crown) chakra, the revealer of all mantras and your connection to higher consciousness.

During the process of creation, *shakti kundalini* descends from the *sahasrara* through all the chakras. As it descends, it causes *maya,* or delusion, ignorance, limitation and obsession with material life. It stops and remains in the *muladhara* chakra from where it remains to sustain the physical body and all its functions.

One of the most important goals of meditation is the awakening of *kundalini* energy. Through dedicated practice and meditation *shakti kundalini* begins to ascend up through the chakras, awakening each along the way. As it ascends, *kundalini* becomes more subtle and reabsorbs all the creativity lost during its descent. This process is called *laya* absorption which is a type of karma dissolution. In this way, *shakti kundalini* eliminates the veils of maya which evaporate like a mirage. As *shakti kundalini* moves home to the *sahasrara* chakra, it removes mental limitations and enhances consciousness such that mental fluctuations settle down and serenity replaces oscillations which brings about eternal bliss and happiness.

Many forms of yoga help prepare you for this awakening. The foundational work in Raja Yoga such as pranayama, involves acquiring the ability to balance prana or life-force flow through the *ida, pingala,* and *sushumna* channels, which in turn becomes the basis for *kundalini* awakening and the union of *shiva* and *shakti.* This brings great joy and peace to the practitioner and is an important part of spiritual realization and progress. However, the awakening of the *kundalini* is best accomplished when supervised by a Guru. This is because when the kundalini begins to awaken, the practitioner goes through experiences that may be counter-intuitive. Kundalini ascension is supposed to impart energy and balance, wisdom and bliss. However, in the beginning, the practitioner may experience aches and pains in the body, emotional fluctuations and a confused mental state during the ascension. These may be a quite natural part of karmic dissolution, but others may be a result of incorrect practices and only a trained Guru should guide the practitioner through any issues in this phase.

Some commonly experienced signs of *kundalini* awakening which can vary in intensity and duration may be:

- Involuntary shakes and shivers
- Feeling of cold within the body
- Intense feelings of pleasure or bliss
- Intense heat in a particular chakra or the spine
- A feeling of things crawling over hands and/or feet
- Striking flows of energy, like electricity in the body
- Spontaneous mudras (hand gestures), asanas (postures), bandhas (locks)
- A sense of uncertainty or confusion about what you are experiencing
- Increase in visions of inner colors and lights
- Spontaneous and abrupt mood swings
- Waves of intellectual, creative, or spiritual insights
- Inner sounds, such as musical instruments, buzzing, roaring, or thunder

An experienced Guru can help you prepare so that you are ready to absorb these sensations and help you through your transformation.

"This hand contains all healing balms, and this makes whole with gentle touch... With these two healers of disease, we stroke thee with a soft caress."

—*Atharva Veda, book 4, hymn 13*

Reiki: The Power of Divine Grace

REIKI HAS BEEN VARIOUSLY DESCRIBED as a form of alternate medicine, a universal energy, a life force, a method for emotional and physical healing among others.

Reiki does mean life force or spiritual energy since it is a compound word made up of the Japanese words:

- Rei, meaning spirit or soul, is a subtle wisdom that permeates everything animate and inanimate. Reiki is defined as "a higher intelligence that guides the creation and functioning of the universe." It is available to guide you whenever you need it.
- Ki, material energy, an inward flowing force that takes you closer to the absolute. Your feelings, emotions and thoughts affect the strength of Ki's flow. Negative feelings and thoughts restrict Ki's flow.

Within Reiki Raja Yoga practice and teaching; however, Reiki is considered to be beyond energy, para energy, or the controller of all energies.

The Veda or yogic traditional texts refer to the concepts of *para shakti* and *param shakti* which can be used to better understand the idea of para energy. *Para shakti* is the essential nature or real form of the Absolute.

Param shakti is the prana that circulates in this universe and also within our body as life force and energy. Success in this Reiki-Raja Yoga and the path to self-realization involves learning to successfully tap into both *para shakti* and *param shakti.*

The movement of *param shakti* is like *Aum* the sound of creation outward from the Absolute, while the movement of *para shakti* is back inward toward the Absolute. These are the two fundamental powers of the universe with *Aum* flowing out from the Absolute during creation and *para shakti* or Divine Grace back inward toward the Absolute during self-realization. Reiki is this inward flow of Divine Grace toward the absolute and so it's a para energy or force because of its direction similar to *para shakti.*

Eventually, advanced practitioners can access *para shakti* to control the *param shakti* and generate various forms of energy as needed. In this way, as you apply Reiki whether through touch or distance healing, you can accumulate the necessary energies for the appropriate type of healing.

Reiki Raja Yoga connects you to *Aum,* the sound of creation, Reiki, the power of Divine Grace, and *kundalini,* the power of Divine Will. Through persistent practice Reiki Raja Yoga allows you to find the balance between exerting effort to exercise your will and how much to surrender to Divine Grace and the flow of life.

The Principles of Reiki

Reiki Masters have created five Reiki principles. Repeating these five principles daily, preferably in the morning, connects you to Reiki energy.

1. Just for today: I will live in the attitude of gratitude.
2. Just for today: I will not fear or worry.
3. Just for today: I will not be angry.
4. Just for today: I will be honest to my own self.
5. Just for today: I will respect all living beings.
   My Guru, Shri Vijay Bansal, added another principle:
6. Just for today: I will not let my ego-personality judge myself.

The essence of Reiki is explained below.

Just for today: The importance of "today" is highlighted in all six principles. Today defines your present. It teaches you to live each and every moment of the day completely; life just becomes a collection of moments. It is easier to make a commitment to these principles for one day at a time rather than making a lofty commitment to follow these throughout your life to come. You will find more success when you affirm and commit to these principles on a daily basis.

I will live in the attitude of gratitude: Reiki encourages you to be thankful, receiving and giving the gift of the universe. You should be thankful about everything in your life—the good, the bad, and the ugly. Being thankful breaks the cycle of misery. If you are going through a bad time or suffering, then it is because of some karma that was performed in the past, which has become the cause of suffering today. If you start brooding over this and blaming others, you just sink deeper into that misery. By being thankful for whatever you have and whatever situation you are in, you break the cycle of misery; you break the influence of that effect on you, and gradually that thought process leads you out of the suffering that you are in. It creates a new cause for good things to happen in your life.

I will not fear or worry: The principles of Reiki encourage you to trust the universe completely. They tell you to let go of your fears and worries, make the best possible efforts, and leave the rest in the hands of the universe. This frees you from your fears, and you start believing in the universe.

Fear begets more fear; worry begets more worry. The moment you stop worrying, you demonstrate your faith in the Absolute, and the moment that demonstration happens, the powers of Reiki (the para shakti) and the powers of prana and Aum (the param shakti) descend on you and begin to support you. So, don't let fear create more fear and don't let worry create more worry. Just for today, live without fear or worry.

I will not be angry: This principle encourages you to stay away from anger and attain perfect balance of emotion and mind through Reiki. It guides you to live a peaceful and calm life.

Anger burns your positive karma and reduces the power of your soul. In some cases, you can be angry about rightful causes. I believe in positive anger as well. However, it has to be channeled correctly. And in all circumstances, it is better to not be angry and think about the situation in a positive manner. This does not mean that you become inert and do not respond to a situation; it simply means that you act with equanimity and understand the situation that you are in. That is the best way to not burn your positive karma and use it to your advantage.

I will be honest to my own self: Reiki shows you how to integrate and utilize the power of honesty for everyday work. It reiterates the importance of work and how working honestly can enable you to lead a meaningful life, growing and learning every day.

Honesty toward your own self is extremely important. When you are honest to your own self, you increase the power of your soul and let it work through your mind and body. Honesty toward your own self aligns your soul, mind, and body. When you are not honest with your own self, you disintegrate. Your chakras start to fall out of alignment, and you are not able to draw the right amount of power from your soul into your mind. This dishonesty to your own self weakens your mind and the power of your soul. Yoga is about alignment and integration of all the chakras, and the first step to do this is to be honest to your own self.

I will respect all living beings: This principle started out as ***"I will be respectful of my parents and elders"***. Over a period of time, this has been expanded into "Just for today, I will respect all living beings." Whatever learning you have achieved is because of your parents and elders, and also people around you. When you interact with people, you learn some things, and you share some good experiences and some bad experiences; you need to respect people for all that they are teaching you. This respect also empowers you to see everybody as your own extended self. This does not mean that you should not be cautious and that you should not apply your judgment when interacting with people; it just means that you act with respect under all circumstances and that you are never hateful or spiteful.

Reiki encourages you to nurture a sense of oneness and love. It mentions that there is one single soul in this universe and this soul does not distinguish between self and others. Therefore, when you are kind to others, you are kind to yourself!

I will not let my ego-personality judge myself: You are constantly judging yourself; you criticize yourself for your follies and praise yourself for the numerous achievements that you make. The criticism specifically weakens or blocks your mind. When you stop judging yourself, you also empower yourself to not judge others. Life is not about judging yourself or judging people around you; it is all about living.

Therefore, Reiki encourages you to not belittle yourself or anyone else. You must not run yourself down in your own eyes or in anyone else's eyes. At the same time, you must also not over elevate yourself. Reiki encourages you to be humble; that way you get free from the clutches of your ego.

Meditating on these principles every single day allows you to live life in a richer way. You can end any meditation session by repeating these six principles.

Practicing Pranayama

Pranayama is derived from two Sanskrit words, *prana* (life), and *ayama* (control). It is the extraction of *prana* from the universe. The sun is the largest source of new prana on this planet. To a yogi, the sun is a *devta* or conscious being, and its light rays are conscious energy or conscious *prana.* In fact, eastern yogis worship the sun, like all nature, as a source of intelligent life force. Through the practice of *pranayama,* yogis extract prana from the universe and circulate it within their bodies.

Some consider *pranayama* as breath control, but this is an incomplete picture. Pranayama is in fact control over prana. Breath is simply the vehicle that transports prana into and out of your body. Pranayama can be thought of as control over the muscular apparatus whose movement causes the movement of the lungs and therefore moves the breath. Muscle power prana is the power source for those muscles.

Pranayama is therefore life control and not breath control. *Prana* is force or energy. In this sense, the universe is filled with *prana*; all creation is a manifestation of force, a play of force.

Pranayama has three parts:

1. Inhaling
2. Restraining (the pause between an inhale and exhale)
3. Exhaling

Through the practice of *pranayama*—offering the inhaling into the exhaling and the exhaling into the inhaling breath (*apana* into *prana* and *prana* into *apana*)—you can recharge the blood and cells with life energy that has been distilled from the breath and reinforced with the pure spiritualized life force in the spine and brain. You attain conscious life force control.

Reiki Raja Yoga combines *pranayama* with meditation using *bija* or seed mantras that you can repeat during the session to help activate chakra energy and flow through the *sushumna* nadi and purify and balance the mind and body.

Pranayama is a type of meditation. It is the practice of refining breathing and awareness of *prana* flow. When you regularly fill your body with prana or life-force energy through these techniques, you begin to develop control of your body and mind. You will learn to control yourself more effectively when you are suddenly filled with tension or sadness or fear and work towards a more stable less oscillating emotional state.

Aum is the most renowned and expansive of the *bija* mantras. It is the seed sound of creation and its chanting causes a surge of spiritual energy. *Aum* destroys negativity and stimulates vitality throughout the body.

Ideally, *pranayama* should be practiced twice daily—early mornings and toward early evenings are best. But remember, it's better to practice sometime during the day than to not practice at all. More regularity and frequency will of course bring greater, more consistent benefits. Your *pranayama* will become more precise as your senses open and expand through regular practice.

Sitting Postures for Pranayama and Meditation

The ideal *asana* (posture) for pranayama is seated down, with your spine erect. You can sit on a cushion on the floor or, if that is too hard, on a chair. You can adopt an effective posture while sitting in a chair, sitting in the lotus position, or sitting cross-legged. But remember, the posture you take can help concentration, or can act as a distraction. It may look really cool to sit cross-legged, but if you don't have the flexibility to sit like that comfortably for an hour, you'll simply suffer! Choose a posture that is right for you. All these postures work; it's important to find one that's comfortable for you.

Seated in a Chair

You can meditate perfectly well in an ordinary dining-room or office chair.

If you can, keep your back straight so that only the base of your spine is touching the back of the chair. Of course, if you can't sustain that, you may need to use the seat-back as an extra support for the duration of meditation.

Support your hands by resting them on your thighs.

If your feet don't reach the floor, use a folded blanket or cushion to prevent your legs from dangling. If your legs are too long, then find another chair, or put a cushion or folded blanket under you to raise you up.

Simple Cross Legged Position

Sitting cross legged is a stable and grounded posture for meditation if you are flexible enough to be comfortable for the duration of the meditation. There are a number of ways of sitting with crossed legs.

If you can't quite get both knees on the floor, then you can use some padding (a thin cushion) under your knee to keep you stable. You can always do some stretching to loosen up your hips, and then come back and try a cross legged posture later.

Hands should be naturally supported in your lap or on your thighs. If your hands can't naturally settle that way, rest them on some cushions to keep them supported. You can also alternate the foot that is in front from time to time.

Lotus Position

This posture is only suitable for those who are flexible or practiced at hatha yoga. If you feel any pain, or this posture becomes uncomfortable, then try a simpler posture.

In full lotus, feet rest on opposite thighs, with soles pointing upwards.

Full lotus is considered the ideal meditating position. Sitting comfortably in full lotus brings you close to the ground with good balanced and symmetry.

Meditating Lying Down: The Corpse Pose

Savasana (lying down or the corpse pose) sets up conditions that allow you to gradually enter a relaxed state which can serve as a starting point for meditation.

Rest your entire body on the floor. Extend your arms and legs outward from the torso evenly and symmetrically.

Mentally scan the body from head to toe, gradually releasing each body part and each muscle group. Notice all the places where the body is making contact with the floor. If you feel uncomfortable in any part of your body, you may need further support. Use props to relieve any pressure and release tension so you can fully relax.

Breathing and Meditation Exercises

Begin all breathing and meditation exercises with a prayer. Thank Divine for all the blessings in all creation. Wish happiness, peace, and health to all beings. Think of your own body as strong and healthy, and believe in the power of your mind to bring positive change to your reality.

You can download a guided meditation track at www.divineheartcenter.com.

Basic Pranayama Breathing

This basic pranayama breathing technique is 5000 years old. It stimulates the *ida* and *pingala nadis* along the spine, generating a deep sense of physical, mental, and emotional well-being and eliminating stress.

Sit comfortably with your spine erect.

Close the right nostril with the thumb and then slowly inhale through the left nostril, repeating the word Aum four times.

Now firmly close both nostrils by placing the forefinger on the left one and hold the breath in, mentally repeating Aum eight times.

Then, removing the thumb from the right nostril, exhale slowly through that, repeating Aum four times. As you close the exhalation, draw in the abdomen forcibly to expel all the air from the lungs.

Now slowly inhale through the right nostril, keeping the left one closed, repeating Aum four times.

Then close the right nostril with the thumb and hold the breath while repeating Aum eight times.

Now unclose the left nostril and slowly exhale, repeating Aum four times, drawing in the abdomen as before.

Repeat this exercise twice in each sitting so you end up doing four pranayamas; two for each nostril.

The Pink Lotus Meditation

The Pink Lotus meditation opens the heart chakra, dissolving fear, pain, and depression from your energy field by placing you in the vibration of divine love.

Sit or lie down comfortably with your spine erect.

Close your eyes and take a few minutes to observe the inflow and outflow of your breath.

Now intend that a beautiful pink lotus is blossoming in your heart.

Imagine cosmic energy is entering from everywhere, especially from up above you, nourishing the lotus.

Imagine the lotus expanding and blooming further; now you become the lotus. Feel it filling you with divine love.

If your attention drifts to thoughts in your mind, sounds in your environment, or sensations in your body, gently return to your breath.

When done, thank the lotus for filling you up with divine love.

The Personal Fire Right Meditation

The Personal Fire Right or *Swayagya* meditation burns off negative energy within the aura and increases will power.

Sit comfortably with the spine erect; do not lie down.

Close your eyes and take a few minutes to observe the inflow and outflow of your breath.

Now intend that an energizing divine fire is emerging from the base of your spine. Feel your physical body, your energy body, and your mind engulfed in this fire.

Imagine this fire is burning out all your negativities, all the negative emotions, pains, past memories, and suffering. This fire energizes you and increases your will power.

Now imagine the fire becomes more and more intense with every passing moment, burning out all the negativities, energizing you, creating a Divine Will power within you, and you are healed.

Thank the divine fire for energizing you. The fire now subsides.

The So Hum Meditation

This simple but powerful technique uses the breath and the *So Hum* mantra to move beyond your mind's busy chatter and cultivate present moment awareness. *So* means "I am," and *Hum* means "that."

Training your breath with the *So Hum* mantra, and moving your mind's focus up and down the *sushumna nadi,* aligns and balances the chakras through which the *sushumna* travels. This brings your mind into a peaceful state in preparation for advancing into deeper meditation.

Sit comfortably with the spine erect; do not lie down.

Close your eyes and take a few minutes to observe the inflow and outflow of your breath.

Now take a slow, deep breath through your nose, while thinking or silently repeating the word So. *Then slowly exhale through your nose while silently repeating the word* Hum.

Continue to allow your breath to flow easily, silently repeating Soooo . . . Hummmm . . . *with each inflow and outflow of the breath.*

If your attention drifts to thoughts in your mind, sounds in your environment, or sensations in your body, gently return to your breath, silently repeating Soooo. . . Hummmm.

Do this process for five minutes to start with then build up to 30 minutes, when you feel ready to sustain your focus.

Mindfulness Meditations

You can begin to balance your chakras by just being mindful.

The Reiki Raja Yoga approach is aimed at activating, unblocking and balancing the chakras, not only for healing purposes, but as a part of the process of self-realization.

Here is a basic mindfulness exercise to begin.

Begin by lying down on the floor on a yoga mat. Tuck your shoulder blades under you. This is important as it makes your chest feel open and broad.

Now, stretch your legs as far as you can and then relax them. Your arms should be placed about one foot from the sides of your body. The palms should be facing up.

Next, detach from your thoughts. Do not try to stop the thoughts from occurring; just try to visualize them, wrap them up, label them, and move ahead, visualizing your wphysical body, surroundings, and awareness overall.

Now that you are detached from your thoughts, you can start the process of awareness or mindfulness.

Begin by bringing your awareness to your root chakra at the base of your spine, visualizing the round, red chakra that is turning like a wheel. You can feel it by just being mindful. Thoughts may come and go. Don't attempt to stop them; just try to visualize and feel your chakra.

Shift your awareness toward your sacral chakra. It may appear like a spinning ball of energy that is orange in color. It is all right if you do not see it yet. Awareness is all about feeling it. Just feel it below your navel and make a mental note of your perceptions.

Now, try to feel each of the remaining chakras. Feel your front solar plexus chakra right below your rib cage (this may appear yellow in color) and your front heart chakra in the center of your chest (this would be pink or green in color). Now shift your mindfulness to your throat chakra, which is blue in color, and then to your third eye chakra, which may appear indigo in color. Lastly, feel your seventh chakra (which may be purple or white in color). Do not attempt to imagine your chakras; just try to feel them.

Once you have felt each of your chakras, move your toes and fingers a little; this is to bring your consciousness back to the physical world.

Now, roll toward the right side and sit up when you feel ready.

Grab a notebook and write down all that you experienced during the exercise. This is important because it will help you track any noticeable patterns with respect to chakras. You should repeat this exercise at least once a week in order to get clarity on the patterns.

Mindfulness exercises call for concentrating your conscious efforts on being aware. You may find this difficult in the beginning. Don't be discouraged if you are unable to perceive your energy centers at this time.

Here is an exercise that you can practice in order to enhance your mindfulness. With focused effort you will be able to tune in to your energy centers!

Sit comfortably with your spine erect. Now, lower your eyes. Your eyes should be at a forty-five-degree angle, preferably half-closed and half-open. Since your eyes are partly open, you will not fall asleep. At the same time you are maintaining your mastery over the physical plane, because you can see what is going on around you.

Don't try to stop your thoughts. They are thoughts; they will keep coming. Just observe them. You can visualize a thought as a gift wrapped up inside a piece of paper and just labeled as "thought."

Now, make yourself aware of your physical body. Notice how your body feels. Let the power of mindfulness guide you to notice and feel each portion of your body. The right shoulder may hurt, and the stomach may feel empty. Do not get up and eat something. Concentrate on feeling each and every sensation.

Visualize these sensations, wrap them up in a piece of paper, and label them "shoulder ache," "empty stomach," and so on.

Next, move to the room around you.

Do not get up and move; just be aware of the room around you. How does the air feel? Can you smell a particular aroma? Does the blanket feel warm? Once again, visualize all that you can feel and wrap it up in a piece of paper—"the aroma of chamomile tea," "cool breeze," and so on.

Finally, come back to your awareness.

Step away from your thoughts, from what you are feeling in your physical body, and from the things happening around you. Let them stay where they are—wrapped up in pieces of paper but not disturbing you.

Try to stay in this state for at least five minutes. Gradually increase the time to about twenty minutes each day.

The Chakra Seed Sounds Meditation

Bija mantras are one-syllable seed sounds that, when said aloud or chanted mentally, activate the energy of the chakras in order to open, heal, and harmonize your chakras. **Important Note:** Mental chanting will take you deeper into the meditation than chanting out loud.

You can chant the *bija* mantras, either one at a time or in sequences. Visualizing the color, location and positive impact of each chakra as you chant the corresponding *bija* mantra will provide you with an added dose of energy.

Here is a simple meditation using the 7 *bija* mantras associated with each chakra:

> *Visualize the root chakra and recite the sound* **"lam."**
>
> *Now, visualize your sacral chakra by reciting* **"vam."**
>
> *Next, boost your solar plexus chakra through the chant of* **"ram."**
>
> *Elevate your heart chakra now using the sound* **"yam."**
>
> *Open your throat chakra by the chant of* **"ham."**
>
> *Now, visualize and enhance your third-eye chakra with the sound of* **"om."**
>
> *And finally, open your crown chakra through visualization and creating an extended sound of* **"om."** *You can also maintain complete silence at this time.*

Throughout this process, focus on visualizing loving and nurturing energy traveling through your body and into the universe. Use the power of affirmations to remind yourself that you can feel this positive energy—you can feel it travel from your root chakra to your crown chakra and then into the universe.

You will be amazed at the balance and harmony that you can achieve by simply practicing this meditation for a few minutes every day.

More Advanced Concepts

Eight Principle Components of Raja Yoga

The eight root principles or stages of Raja Yoga are:

1. Yama
2. Niyama
3. Asana
4. Pranayama
5. Pratyahara
6. Dharana
7. Dhyana
8. Samadhi

The first two are a complementary pair of ethical rule sets, sort of a Hindu equivalent of the commandments. The Yamas are things not to do and Niyamas are things to do.

Yama

Yama is about self-control. It comprises five not-to-do things:

Ahimsa, or non-violence, basically is a directive to not kill, cause pain, or harm to anyone in words or deeds. Incidentally, this is the one that keeps most Raja yogis vegetarian because the killing of an animal is seen as breaking this directive.

Satya or truthfulness is the equivalent of "thou shalt not lie," and directs you to speak the truth with love.

Asteya is basically, thou shalt not steal." However, here it extends to mental images, and feelings as well as physical objects. Do not steal hope or joy, or opportunity from anyone.

Brahmacharya suggests restraint or abstinence, it means pursuing *Brahman* or the state of ultimate reality. It denotes celibacy before marriage and faithfulness during marriage. However, in a modern western sense it can be viewed as devotion to learning when young and focus on spiritual liberation when older without distractions from the physical appetites. This is not taken to mean a neglect of normal intimacy in the course of a modern life, but a prioritizing of commitment to Divine and the physical disciplines of yogic practice.

Aparigraha is the directive against avarice and rapacity. It's about letting go of excess and possessing only what is needed and experiencing the liberation associated with letting go of covetousness.

Niyama

Niyama is about discipline during action. It comprises five to-dos for positive and healthy living:

First is the principle of *Shauca* or purity of mind and body. It emphasizes purity in everything from your thoughts to the clothes on your back and the people that you associate with who can influence you in a positive manner.

Next is *Santosh* or contentment or satisfaction. It is living with the realization that all worldly goods are eventually a source of disappointment and only the experience of inner wealth and inner satisfaction brings holistic happiness.

Tapa or self-discipline is about exercising control over yourself to continue on a chosen path despite life's challenges using patience, determination and perseverance as requisite virtues.

Svadhyaya connotes introspective study of self, through the study of the scriptures. Reading the ancient *vedas* is a tremendous guide for a yogi from the beginning through to mastery and beyond. Consistent reading and reciting of the Yoga Sutras, the Upanishads, or the Bhagavad Gita, imparts a wealth of knowledge and wisdom.

Ishvarapranidhana is composed of two words *ishvara* meaning supreme being or God, and *pranidhana* devotion, commitment and surrender to Divine.

Asana

Asana in Sanskrit means to sit down or sitting down. In yoga *Asana* refers to the posture or sitting position that a yogi adopts. According to the *Yoga Sutras, Patanjali*, an *asana* is a seated position that is relaxed but firm, or a comfortable and steady posture. This component refers to the need to exercise daily in a comfortable meditative posture. You should choose the easiest posture that you can maintain comfortably for the duration of your practice. Your spine must be held free and upright such that your head, neck, and chest are in a straight line. This step enables you to establish control over your body. Daily exercise is critical to your progress along the Reiki Raja Yoga path.

Pranayama

See Practicing Pranayama.

Pratyahara

Pratyahara, is the practice of sensory withdrawal. Yogis strive to be able to direct their senses at will. During this stage yogis learn to withdraw the five physical senses of smell, sight, hearing, taste and touch, such that they don't reach the brain and instead focus their consciousness inward in order to reach the next three of the eight components of Raja Yoga.

In the *pranayama* stage, you learn to bring *prana* into your body. Since *prana* drives the senses, during *pratyahara,* you learn to further control *prana* flow more precisely and in fact, focus it on a single point instead of wasting it on the senses.

Dharana

Dharana comes from the root word *dhri* meaning to maintain or hold. *Dharana* is the art of concentration. At this stage, you can hold your mind focused on a certain point. You can for example feel nothing but the sole of your left foot and no other part of your body. In *dharana,* you may focus and feel only your heart, or a lotus in place of your heart. As you continue and your practice gets deeper, your perceptions become finer; the sound of a pin drop may appear like bolt of thunder. In this way, you will be able to concentrate all your thoughts on a single particular object.

Dhyana

Dhyana is the state of contemplative meditation reflecting on anything on which your mind is focused. All meditative techniques only serve as preliminary exercises to help reach this state. Dhyana takes many years of committed and dedicated practice to accomplish. When you reach this stage, your ego ceases to exist and you become one with the absolute. Yogis at this stage develop complete control over their minds and experience pure being.

Samadhi

Samadhi means bringing or joining together. At this final stage of yoga, the act of knowledge, the object of knowledge and the knower unite and the distinction between them dissolves away such that there is only oneness. We are aware of two states, unconsciousness and consciousness. There is a third state of complete realization called super consciousness which is samadhi. It is a higher state of existence beyond reason.

Closing Thoughts

Reiki Raja Yoga is a practice that strives toward the gift of Divine Grace and the wisdom of Divine Will. Practicing Reiki Raja Yoga at least once a day can help you begin to calm the *vrittis* or swirling thoughts in your mind. The calm and restrained mind is the foundation upon which to begin your journey toward holistic happiness and self-realization which are the ultimate goal of Reiki Raja Yoga.

Reiki Raja Yoga is an authentic, all-inclusive, nondenominational and flexible path. It begins with self-effort and works through regular practice. If you begin to make it part of your life, it can help transform your material and spiritual world. So, go out and begin with peace and love in your heart.

GLOSSARY

Ahamkar
See *Ego.*

Anahata Chakra
See *Heart Chakra.*

Ananda
Pure bliss or the essence of life; the realization that life itself is bliss.

Atman
The soul or eternal self.

Aum
The seed sound of creation. Its chanting causes a surge of spiritual energy, destroys negativity, and stimulates vitality throughout the body.

Aura
An energy field that surrounds and extends out of your physical body. It is generated by the chakras, seven vortices of energy spinning inside your body along your spine. See *Kosha.*

Avidya
A limited state of mind or spiritual ignorance.

Bhakti

The power of devotion. One of two Divine powers that make holistic happiness possible. When you are devoted and exercise your will positively, you bring about kripa or divine grace, which in turn harnesses the unlimited power of shakti or divine will.

Bija Mantras

One syllable seed sounds that, when said aloud or chanted mentally, activate the energy of the chakras in order to open, heal, and harmonize your chakras.

Chakras

Seven vortices of energy spinning inside your body along your spine.

Chit

The peaceful, complete, and unbroken consciousness of you being life itself and not simply who you happen to be in this life.

Crown Chakra

Located at the top of your head and extending out is the seat of your universal self, the crown (sahasrara) chakra. This is the center of wisdom, self-realization, and pure consciousness.

Divine Grace

See *Bhakti.*

Divine Will

See *Shakti.*

Ego

Pride about oneself; the root of all unhappiness.

Heart Chakra

Located inside the sushumna nadi, at the level of the heart, is the heart (anahata) chakra. This is the middle chakra with the three worldly chakras below it and the three spiritual chakras above. The heart chakra is the connection between the two sides and allows you to balance your spiritual qualities with your physical.

Holistic Happiness

A state of physical, emotional, and spiritual health that permeates all aspects of your life, from your relationships to your financial well-being. When your body, mind, and spirit are happy at once.

Ida Nadi

One of two nadis that wraps itself around the sushumna nadi. Ida conducts a cooling, calm receptive and meditative energy or what the Chinese call yin.

Karana Sarira

In Hinduism, the human being is composed of three bodies where the five koshas (sheaths) reside: the gross body (sthula sarira), subtle body or astral body (linga sarira), and causal body (karana sarira). The karmic data imprinted into your causal body or karana sarira leads to your life as you find it.

Karma

The word karma means work, deed, or action, and describes actions as well as their resultant energy. Karma governs our environment and our physical and spiritual inheritance. In Hinduism, there are three types of karma: sanchita, prarabdha, and khriyamana. Reiki Raja Yoga helps you to dissolve and thereby alter your karma.

Kosha

A sheath or covering of the self. There are five koshas: the annamaya kosha—physical sheath, pranmaya kosha—energy sheath, manomaya kosha—emotional sheath, gyanmaya kosha—mental/intellectual sheath, and anandmaya kosha—causal sheath or the radiance of the soul. The second, third, and fourth koshas make up the human aura. For simplicity, some western teachings consider all five to be the aura.

Kripa

See *Divine Grace.*

Kriyamana Karma

The karma you produce in your current life and the way your actions and thoughts in this life contribute to your sanchita karma.

Kundalini
An energy located in the base of the spine that, in one of its manifestations, sustains the physical body and its functions from within the muladhara or root chakra. Hindu scripture describes three expressions of the kundalini: para-kundalini, prana-kundalini, and shakti-kundalini.

Mahavir
The most powerful of warriors and yogis.

Manipura Chakra
See *Solar Plexus Chakra.*

Maya
A subtle, limiting, collective principle in creation that hides your true identity from your conscious mind.

Muladhara Chakra
See *Root Chakra.*

Nadis
Energy channels running along your body. According to ancient Indian scriptures, there are 72,000 nadis. The three most important nadis, through which prana flows, are called sushumna, ida, and pingala.

Para-Kundalini
The unmanifested cosmic energy.

Para Shakti

Beyond energy. Divine Grace, the essential nature or real form of the Absolute.

Param Shakti

Supreme pranic power. The prana that circulates in this universe and also within our body as life force and energy.

Pingala Nadi

One of two nadis that wraps itself around the sushumna nadi. Pingala conducts a heating, active, forceful, get-it-done energy or yang in Chinese philosophy.

Personal Energy

The energy necessary for your personal well-being. Your personal energy is made up of the aura and the chakra system.

Prana

A universal energy that nourishes and connects life. Humans are surrounded by a field comprised of this energy, which links the physical and spiritual worlds.

Prana-Kundalini

The vital energy of the created universe.

Pranayama

A type of meditation. It is the practice of refining breathing and awareness of prana flow. When you regularly fill your body with prana or life-force energy, you begin to develop control of your body and mind.

Prarabdha Karma

The portion of your sanchita karma allotted to you for this lifetime. It's the karma that is ready for you to tackle and understand. There are two subcategories: sthaanbaddh and samaybaddh. Sthaanbaddh karma manifests only in a particular place. Samaybaddh karma manifests only at or after a certain time.

Raja Yoga

The practice of learning to use the mind to objectively observe the world around you and to understand its transitory yet clinging nature.

Reiki

A universal energy used for emotional and physical healing. Within Reiki Raja Yoga practice and teaching; however, Reiki is considered to be beyond energy. It is para energy or the controller of all energies. See *Para Shakti* and *Param Shakti.*

Reiki Raja Yoga

The union of two ancient practices, one a healing system, the other a meditative system. The goal of Reiki Raja Yoga is to apply techniques that remove blockages and imbalances in the chakras, and to focus, tame, and purify the mind. The practice of Reiki Raja Yoga cultivates holistic happiness and self-realization.

Root Chakra
Located inside the sushumna nadi, at the base of the spine, the root (muladhara) chakra is your foundation or earth chakra. Feelings related to safety, survival, and security emerge from this center.

Sacral Chakra
Four to six finger widths above the root chakra, and below the level of the navel, is the sacral (svadhisthana) chakra. The sacral chakra is the seat of your lower self and home of instant gratification. It drives the ego's immediate goals.

Sahasrara Chakra
See *Crown Chakra.*

Sanchita Karma
The totality of your karma present at your birth and responsible for all your rebirths that goes back through all time to original creation.

Sat
Eternal consciousness, the essence of life or the amount of life that is inside you.

Satchitananda

A compound Sanskrit word that means the ultimate state of spiritual evolution. Satchitananda is realized after a lifetime of practice, unflinching faith, surrender, and determined effort.

Shakti

The power of divine will. One of two Divine powers that make holistic happiness possible. When you are devoted and exercise your will positively, you bring about kripa or divine grace, which in turn harnesses the unlimited power of divine will.

Shakti-Kundalini

The eternal foundation of bliss flowing from the crown (sahasrara) chakra, the revealer of all mantras, and your connection to higher consciousness. Also, the intermediary between the other two expressions of kundalini: para-kundalini and prana-kundalini.

Social Energy

The energy of people with whom you interact with daily.

Solar Plexus Chakra

Located inside the sushumna nadi, at the level of the solar plexus, is the solar plexus (manipura) chakra where your power to achieve springs.

Spatial Energy
The energy levels predominant in your working space (factory, shop, or office) and living space (home). These energy levels are termed vastu energies in Sanskrit.

Spirit
The aspect of humanness that connects with the Absolute, Divine, or God.

Spirituality
The practice of unfolding yourself layer-by-layer to ultimately realize the inexhaustible spirit overflowing with pure unlimited love and dazzling with infinite intelligence.

Sushumna Nadi
The sushumna nadi begins at the first chakra and ends at the seventh. It is the body's most important energy channel because it carries kundalini energy from the base of the spine to the crown of the head, imparting self-realization.

Svadhisthana Chakra
See *Sacral Chakra.*

Third Eye Chakra
Located inside the sushumna nadi, between the eyebrows, is the third eye (ajna) chakra. Ajna is Sanskrit for command and the third eye chakra is the command center of the mind and body.

Throat Chakra
Located inside the sushumna nadi, at the level of the throat, is your throat (vishuddha) chakra, the seat of patience, understanding, and self-expression.

Vastu Healing
The healing of the spiritual and mental energy field of your home, office, shop, and other premises using powerful instruments or yantras, such as gem stones, pyramids, and Rudraksha beads.

Vishuddha Chakra
See *Throat Chakra.*

AUTHOR BIOGRAPHY

Shailesh Kumar is a modern guru who has uniquely integrated the two practices of Reiki and Raja Yoga. Shailesh was initiated into the Reiki lineage of Sensei Mikao Usui and the Kriya Yoga lineage of Mahavatar Babaji by his guru, the late Shri Vijay Bansal.

As founder of the Divine Heart Center, an organization dedicated to the philosophy and practice of holistic happiness and self-realization, Shailesh has introduced thousands of seekers to Reiki Raja Yoga throughout the world.

Made in the USA
Middletown, DE
16 May 2019